Distributed by

ℙ

Pisgah Press, LLC
PO Box 9663, Asheville, NC 28715-0663

Pisgah Press was established in 2011 to publish and promote
works of quality offering original ideas and insight into the human condition and the world around us.

Cover and book design by Westleigh Heath

Library of Congress Control Number: 2022944742

ISBN: 978-1-942016-69-4

Printed in the United States of America
First Printing
September 2022

Acting Onstage

55

Practical

Tips

for

Success

by

C. Robert Jones

For
Ursula Kunisch

————

Actor, Teacher, Friend,
whose consistent belief in my work
has always been an inspiration.

————————

Edited by Wes Heath

Why This Book?

There have been many books written about acting, particularly about styles, great performances, and biographies of actors themselves. This book is not about any of those. It focuses on some of the practical things that actors should know in order to make their work flow more smoothly, especially actors new to the craft. It deals with the nitty-gritty, the tools that will help to create a dynamic and memorable performance. It also provides an avenue for how to think and also how to build a successful theatre persona that inspires, engenders confidence, and elevates you above your peers. While it might be a primer for some actors, I hope it will be a "refresher" for those who have been "at it" for a long time.

I began my theatre career as an actor, and I'm very grateful my entry into the wonderful world of theatre started that way. It gave me a leg-up in understanding how actors "tick" and most of all, how they work to create fascinating characters. I've had the same doubts, fears, passions, questing, frustrations, and elations that all actors have, and I've experienced some aspect of all the things I'm writing about—things you won't always find in a book.

How did it begin? Simply. I got asked. A small theatre company in Washington, DC was looking for a young man to play Jack Chesney in a forthcoming production of the British comedy classic, *Charley's Aunt*. I had the right look for the part, so the director took a chance and cast me even though he knew I'd never been in a play before.

In the next several weeks, I was given a crash course in acting. I made every mistake possible, but I was nurtured with care by the director and the other "old pros" in the cast.

By opening night, I had become Jack Chesney. I had had no time to think about any of it. I just did it. I got lucky, however, because the production was seen by well-known theatre director, Pauline Eaton Oak, who ran her own summer theatre in Washington. She asked me to join the group, and for the next four summers, I had the best acting apprenticeship in town—on-the-job training. She cast me in all kinds of roles, pushing me to stretch my technique and my talent. Despite the wonderful experience I was getting, I knew I needed more consistent and disciplined formal training, so after the second season, I began MFA theatre studies at The Catholic University of America there in DC.

With degree in hand, I gradually moved into playwriting and directing, working with actors, from four to eighty whose training ranged from zilch to post graduate. My directing work took me to college and university campuses, to community theatres, and to professional companies. Along the way, I kept noticing little things (and often BIG things) –all fixable—which got in the way of actors' smooth sailing from auditions through rehearsals to performances. I began to make a list of them, and that's the material that comprises this book. I reason that a well-prepared and secure actor gives a richer performance, thus giving audiences a more satisfying experience. So, onward and upward in search of excellence!

I hope these tips bring you a deeper appreciation of the process of acting, a mastery of the craft, and also provide success unbounded. Enjoy!

C. Robert Jones

Terms for Actors

Amateur—From the Latin root word, "to love." So, literally, when we speak of an amateur actor who works with a community theatre, we know the actor (and mostly everybody else) is participating as a pastime, for enjoyment. The actor may have little or no training and is not being paid. The word has a pejorative connotation, too. To be called an amateur when you are a well-trained professional is not a compliment. If often relates to bad behavior or thoughtless conduct. Sometimes it can refer to a self-indulgent performance which distorts the credibility of the character and the play.

Professional—Usually means an actor is being paid to perform, implying a background of formal training and a résumé of acting roles, but not always. Actors' Equity Association is the union for actors and stage managers. Not all professional companies are Equity houses, however. Any actor, regardless of status, who is called a "Pro" is receiving a very high compliment. The term often refers to conduct, attitude, or superior talent in creating a memorable performance.

Non-professional—Usually means the actor is not being paid and is non-Equity.

Unprofessional—Refers to behavior or attitude which is not conducive to upholding the highest ethical and professional standards of theatre.

TABLE OF CONTENTS

TABLE OF CONTENTS

Blocking/movement

Lights

Props

Hair

Costumes

Generic Concerns

Curtain Calls

Acknowledgments

Acting Onstage

55

Practical

Tips

for

Success

Acting!
It's just telling a story.

Everybody loves a story!

Even from our earliest days, we say: "Read me a story." The adventures of others in faraway places stimulate our imaginations. It explains the popularity of plays, films, and fiction in general. Getting away from it all can be fun, restorative, and even life-changing.

One can imagine in primitive historic ages the ritual of story-telling by a narrator alone. This morphs into people suddenly "becoming" the characters in the sagas. They talk and move around as real people, and so theatre, in its simplest forms, begins. Acting, then, is trying to make an audience believe we are somebody else. Of course, there must be a willing suspension of disbelief. We know the person is pretending, but after a bit, we forget that. If the actor is good, we'll believe anything he says or does. That's the goal of all actors.

Harrison Ford (on acting): "I'm an assistant storyteller."

Acting can be a pastime, a craft, and sometimes an art. The talent for it is probably a gift of DNA genes—just like aptitudes for science, music, and art. Can it be taught? Certainly, the craft can, and that craft becomes the common denominator of all actors as they work in groups (casts) to tell a wonderful, believable story.

What, then, are some of the things you, the actor, can do to make the creating characters easier and more successful? Here are some tips:

Tip # 1

Theatre is teamwork.

Start with the understanding that theatre is a collaborative art. It takes many different talents and skills to build a solid production. Actors don't do it by themselves. Think of it this way: It's not about me; it's about us! A violinist can do a concert with just a violin and some music. An artist can have an art show with paintings hanging on a wall. And she doesn't even have to be there. A play, on the other hand, requires actors; a director; set, costume, and lighting folks; a properties master, etc. to show up at an agreed-upon time "to tell a story." We all are dependent on each other. We sink or swim together—no matter how great the stars in a cast may be. We all are part of an ensemble which can't produce the best product unless each participant carries his weight with equal conviction.

John Kander: "There is a kind of classlessness in the theater. The rehearsal pianist, head carpenter, the stage manager, the star of the show—all are family."

Tip # 2

Park your ego (and other "baggage") at the door!

This advice is actually printed on a sign over several backstage entrances around the country. Perhaps you've seen it at a theatre near you. Such a notice is a reminder that you are there to serve the interests of a play as part of an ensemble. Not everybody will be interested in your social media updates. Any actor who uses up all the oxygen in the room is not likely to win friends and influence people in the cast, especially when energies and focus need to be on the production—and not on any individual. Many a show has lost its life at the altar of someone with a giant ego. The TV show graveyard is full of them. Be aware that such folks take everybody else down with them. Never a diva be—and beware of those who are.

James Earl Jones: "No one asked me to be an actor, so no one owed me. There was no entitlement."

Auditions

Actors audition (try out) for a show because they want to be in it. Simple. The objective is to get a role. To do that, you must be seen, heard, understood, and most of all, *BE REMEMBERED*! How?

Tip # 3

Have an audition plan, a strategy, and professional-looking résumé. Leave nothing to chance.

Think of it as a job interview or a contest (which it really is)—and you've got something to win. A role! Find out what you can about the theatre, the director, and the producers (if you don't already know). Be sure you know the production dates and that you are available on those dates. On the audition sheet, be honest about yourself, and don't inflate your résumé. (That kind of information can easily be verified.) Be sure your contact information is accurate and up-to-date (without hand-written corrections) and contains a recent headshot. It's always wise to have back-up contact info and extra copies of your résumé. Be sure to list your unusual abilities. Many actors have gotten jobs when a director discovered they could juggle, ride a unicycle, or speak Russian and French. Keep your résumé relevant to your professional work. Personal information (like marital status, religion, politics, etc.) may

3

not be helpful. If you don't have a résumé, Google "theatre audition résumé" for sample templates.

Amy Schumer (about an audition): "I just treat it like a rehearsal . . . like I already have the job and I'm just going to rehearsal."

Tip # 4
Read the play.

Be curious. Read the script, and if it's not available, find out who the director is looking for: specific characters (or character types) and their ages. It might be a waste of time to audition if all the characters are over 50, and you are 25. If the play is a period piece, go to the Internet and research the manners, mores, and customs of the era—and the setting of the play. You might get clues concerning accents, movement characteristics, etc. which you can use in your audition.

Olivia Colman: "If the script is good, everything you need is in there. I just try to do it honestly."

Tip # 5
Have a prepared piece (memorized).

In most general auditions (where anybody can audition), actors are usually expected to have a memorized monologue, though often at community and academic theatres, they may be asked just to read something from the script itself. Even in that case, prepare something of a minute's duration, memorize it, and ask to do it when called on. If you've read the play, a monologue featuring the character you wish to play may be a wise choice. It gives the director a chance to see how you envision the character . . . and may, indeed, provide a whole new view of how the part might be cast and played. When casting a production of the musical, *Rivals*, the director had in mind an older dowager type actress for the role of Mrs. Malaprop until a younger, pencil-thin actress did her excellent audition.

Steve Martin: "Be so good they can't ignore you."

Tip # 6

Plan what to wear.

Being neat, clean, and well-groomed can be important. Evaluate what you wear carefully. Anything which deviates too far from the norm may make you memorable, but it could also define you in a negative way. For example, a sexually-provocative outfit may make the viewer wonder what you are trying to sell. One of the classic stories about "what to wear at an audition" happened at the audition for the part of Mayella Ewell, the poor white girl who accuses a young black man of rape in the film version of *To Kill a Mockingbird*. Actress Collin Wilcox recalls, "At the audition, all the other girls trying out for the part were overly made up; they had curly, clean hair and wore brassieres and high heels. I wore a secondhand dress, tennis shoes with holes in them, and dirty little white socks. I rubbed cold cream through my hair—that's why my hair looked so dirty." She got the part! Of course, it was her talent that cinched the deal, but she always thought her outfit at the audition got the attention that made it easier.

Kim Cattrall (when auditioning for films): "They said I had to lose weight, let my hair grow, and buy some dresses. I was nailing auditions with my readings, but they wouldn't hire me because I wasn't putting on the glam. It just didn't occur to me."

Tip # 7

Check out the audition space beforehand.

"Why?" you ask. Auditions can be held in any space, and most actors never think about that aspect of the process. They should. I once attended a Southeastern Theatre Conference general audition of upwards of 500 people. It was held in a hotel ballroom with a small stage at the end of the room, backed by black curtains. Representatives from several dozen theatre companies, looking for actors for summer seasons and academic programs, sat at tables around the ballroom. The great advantage of this is that an actor's audition can be seen by many companies at the same time. It can set up a competitive jockeying for the best actors. The small stage was poorly lit, and the overwhelming problem for many of the actors who wore dark blue or black outfits was that they got lost in the curtains. I once saw an ill-conceived production of *The Last of Mrs. Lincoln*, a play about Mary Todd Lincoln after the death of her husband. It was played against black curtains and Mrs. Lincoln wore a black dress. Disaster. Carrying an extra, bright-color jacket, sweater, or overshirt with you (if you haven't seen the space) might come in handy. Leave nothing to chance, remember.

Tip # 8

Using movement at the audition? Yes or no?

It really depends on the nature of the piece. Some movement can be helpful for visual variety and to show your body as it moves in space. You don't want to appear "wooden"—or, conversely, use too much unmotivated movement and appear uncertain or nervous. Let the piece motivate the movement, and remember that some kind of movement, hooked to the text, can be an effective way to let the auditors know the piece is over. Don't let the audition just "die." Plan judiciously. Own the space. When you walk on that stage, it's yours—at least for a minute. Claim it, think it, and dare anyone to take it away from you.

Tip # 9
Wear the same clothes at callbacks.

Although all actors would like to think they are totally memorable, that's not realistic. Especially in large, general auditions. Directors often remember how they first saw an actor. "She's the girl in the green sweater." "He's the guy who wore the black leather vest." They'll expect to see you looking the same when they ask you to callbacks. This includes keeping the same hair style—especially the women. It's just a quirk of the business.

Tip # 10
Keep a record of the audition.

Serious actors who audition frequently, particularly in large cities, keep diaries, notebooks, or computer spreadsheets with the following kinds of audition information:

SHOW _____

Date of audition: _____   Time: _____

Place: _____   Role: _____

Director/Producer: _____   Phone: _____

Address: _____   email: _____

Expenses: (Transportation) _____
(Meals) _____   (Other) _____

Thank you note sent (date): _____
To: _____

What I wore to this audition: _____

Remember that theatre is a business, too. Some of this information can be very helpful at income tax time.

Auditioning for Musicals

Gone are the days when the big musicals used to have the separate components of actors, singing chorus, and dancing ensemble. Today, you're expected to do it all: sing, dance, and act—even though your primary training may have been in only one of those areas. Of course, there are still dancing and singing choruses, depending on a show's content, but actors also have to think about being versatile in their training and in broadening their casting possibilities.

Tip # 11

Choose the right songs.

It's always wise to have two memorized songs ready for any audition: a ballad and an up-tempo song. Both should show your voice range and your voice strengths. Know the songs well, so you can own them. Choose songs that are similar in genre to the music in the show. An opera aria or a hymn probably won't cut it if you are auditioning for *Cabaret*. Should you sing a song from the show itself? Maybe, but there'll probably be others singing the same song, thus inviting comparison. In the same vein, I always advise singers <u>not</u> to sing signature songs of well-known singers (like "Over the Rainbow"—Judy Garland, and "People" — Barbra Streisand). Once again, this invites comparison, and it's probably not going to be helpful to your cause. Singing a song that's not well-known and even unknown can often be a "plus." Directors get tired of hearing the same songs over and over. If one should ask you, "What's that from?", you may have created more interest in yourself. Being able to say, "I wrote it!" raises your stock even further.

Stephen Sondheim: "I was essentially trained by Oscar Hammerstein to think of songs as one-act plays—to move a song from point A to point B dramatically."

A good song, then, probably tells a story—and you're an actor. So, you're not just going to stand and "sing" words. You're going to act a little play, which just happens to be sung.

Tip # 12

Bring your own sheet music.

You wouldn't go skating without skates, and you should never go to a musical audition without bringing your own sheet music. Further, clearly mark the section you intend to use for the audition—and show that to the pianist. Sometimes, in large auditions, you're given only about thirty seconds. Plan to sing the whole song, but don't be surprised if you hear a "Thank you!" before it's over. Know the key of your song, in case the accompanist for some reason has to improvise—and asks. Don't hand the accompanist a big book of songs that won't stay open on the music rack. Always think of the person who's helping to make you look good. People notice—not only your kindness but your professionalism.

Tip # 13

Bring your binder of audition songs.

What is this binder, you ask? Most singers who audition frequently carry with them a collection of sheet music for the songs they can sing in callbacks when they are asked: "Do you have something else?" Usually, the binder is as simple as a folder or a three-ring notebook of music you know well, covering all kinds of genres: Broadway, opera, church, golden oldies, operetta, country, comedy, etc. A former student of mine told me once at an audition, a director noticed her binder, and she ended up beside the piano singing through her book, including a Gilbert and Sullivan operetta song. Just so happened the director was planning a Gilbert and Sullivan production in an upcoming season. The actor's stock went up immediately. She had auditioned for one show but then had a favored position for being cast in a future production. Win-win.

Tip # 14

Handling large auditions

Almost every actor at some point has auditioned in a situation where literally hundreds of others are also auditioning. It's a situation fraught with tension and nerves—and usually you have a minute to dazzle directors—or a minute and a half if you do a monologue and sing part of a song. Sitting through two days of these auditions can be numbing for a director and paralyzing for actors and singers. Formats vary. Actors usually see only the auditions of actors in their smaller groups of, say, 25 or 30, so they are not exposed to the whole mass of other competitors. Actors are given numbers to affix to their chests so they can be seen in a large room setting. The auditors have copies of the résumés (including head shots) and actor numbers so they can be looking at these simultaneously. (Audition formats and variables like weather or health alerts can cause changes. Be sure to verify the latest.)

Often these auditions, particularly in regions away from New York, take place in a large hotel or convention complex where the various theatre companies have reserved space. Everything is essentially under one roof for the sake of efficiency. Companies wanting to call back actors they're interested in are able to set up interviews and perhaps additional auditions quickly. The format works pretty well.

This private meeting is a "Getting to Know You" session among directors, producers, and actors. You, wearing the same audition outfit, may be asked to repeat your audition piece or do a contrasting one. This is indeed where the most important part of the audition takes place. Besides talent, you are being judged on personality, suitability for this particular company, and on your potential for working in an ensemble setting. It's also a chance for the director to gain a broader sense of your versatility, especially if a season of several shows is involved. It's also your opportunity to ask questions. This is expected and can reveal your seriousness about being a part of the company. Usually, you'll be told when a decision will be made, and often contracts are offered on the spot. If you have other offers, this may be the time to mention it. Your stock rises when it's known you're "hot," and if they want you badly enough, they'll likely negotiate.

Paula Abdul: "When you go to an audition and you fail to prepare, prepare to fail."

Rehearsals

Tip # 15

One director, one vision

"A house divided against itself cannot stand."

"You can't have two footballs at a football game." (Where does one look?)

11

Let's assume you've been cast in a play. It's important at the outset to remember that the vision/concept of the production belongs to the director. The buck stops there. It is unprofessional to offer directions to others about their performances. Different opinions and observations can be helpful—it's a collaborative undertaking, for sure—but those should be filtered through the director first.

In his delightful book, *No Pickle, No Performance*, Harold J. Kennedy tells of a Broadway production of *The Front Page* he was getting ready to direct:

"The first rehearsal was called at noon at the Ethel Barrymore Theatre and exactly at twelve o'clock I had the whole company seated on folding chairs lined across the stage.

'We have twelve stars above the title of this play, and a total cast of twenty-four actors. And that's how it's going to be. Twenty-four actors, but only one director. The best way to destroy this play is to have twenty-four separate opinions about how to do it. I know how to do it. And if you find out that I don't, then get together and get me fired. But don't give me any arguments.'"

His point was that actors like authority and respect it. A disciplined cast and a tightly organized structure can make a happy production.

Tip # 16

Keep your own counsel.

Wherever there are groups of people, there are likely to be factions—separate camps—and inevitably, gossip. Play casts are not exempt. While such shenanigans can be harmless, almost all actors who've been around for a while have experienced a production where the backstage atmosphere is toxic, with actors speaking to each other only on stage. For long-run shows with the director no longer around, this can be an uphill slog, taking all the joy out of the craft and the performances. A good motto backstage might be: "Take the high road, and mind your own business."

Tip # 17

Be prompt.

Be on time. It's that simple. It's rude to keep others waiting. If you are unavoidably late, just say, "I'm late, and I apologize." Nobody is interested why.

Tip # 18

Be prepared.

This means "ready to work" at the appointed hour—not just arriving at the rehearsals at the designated time. Scripts and pencils are at the ready, warm-ups are already done, and you are wearing the appropriate rehearsal clothes and shoes. It also means being prepared to show something new since the last rehearsal—moving forward in your own creation and mastery of the character.

Tip # 19

Be amiable, collegial.

You may be having a rotten day, personally, but in truth, while the whole cast and crew might be sympathetic, they are really only interested in what you are contributing to the project at this particular rehearsal. It's as easy to be happy and upbeat as it is to be a misanthrope or a malcontent. You're an actor! Decide to be amiable. Being labelled as argumentative or difficult may hinder chances for future work.

Tip # 20

Tech rehearsals

Tech rehearsals are the ones that test all your patience and professionalism. You've worked for days to get the play on its feet. Now, you're close to opening, feeling good about your performance, your timing, and the show. And then, that momentum is tested as the final set pieces and props are added, lights are set, and costumes appear. Know in advance that these rehearsals are going to be long and tedious, but don't let that stop you from continuing to work. There's likely to be much repetition, trials, and lots of "error," and it will be difficult to get a sense of the show as cues for lights, sound, entrances, etc. are run and re-run. And don't panic if you have to make adjustments. Everybody else will be doing it, too. These are the rehearsals where the crews pull together their work (which has usually been going on somewhere else while you are rehearsing). This time is shared time—actors and crews—learning how everyone must work together. Be sure to stay close by (you'll be needed). Don't talk! Listen and watch! Your cues are likely to be affected. Be cooperative and don't complain. Be professional.

Lines

Tip # 21

Learn lines quickly and as written. Don't paraphrase.

Learn your lines quickly! Everything depends on line security. Your fellow actors are expecting you to give them the lines as written—not an approximation or the gist of the line. Your accuracy affects their own line delivery, their timing, and ultimately their performance. That's basic homework. Actors Equity etiquette says it this way: "As the performance wears on, you may feel that you understand the character better than the playwright. You don't, so quit making up lines."

A good doctor doesn't prescribe a medication that 'sorta' works; he goes for the one that's best for the situation. Nothing annoys a playwright more than hearing a paraphrase of a line for which she's worked diligently to find the right words and rhythm. The cardinal sin is to paraphrase with incorrect grammar. You can bet there'll be a writer somewhere sticking a pin in a doll with your name on it.

Finally, while you, the actor, might learn the lines as written, it's very possible to miss the full intent of lines by falling into the trap of reciting them rather than acting them (Heaven forbid!) by using the wrong phrasing, wrong inflections in words, or wrong timing. Having the words firmly in your brain is just the beginning step of building a believable character.

Tip # 22

Emphasize the correct word(s) for the clearest understanding of the story.

In the following sentence are seven words. See what happens when each is emphasized:

YOU can lead a horse to water. (Implying I can't.)

You CAN lead a horse to water. (Meaning you're able to do that chore.)

You can LEAD a horse to water. (But you can't drive him or force him there.)

You can lead A horse to water. (But not two or three horses.)

You can lead a HORSE to water. (But not a billy goat, perhaps.)

You can lead a horse TO water. (But not away from once you've got him there.)

You can lead a horse to WATER. (But not to beer or apple juice.)

Seven different interpretations of that sentence. Sometimes a script writer will underline or italicize a word to be sure the actor knows the intended interpretation. Usually, however, the interpretation of lines is left to the actors. They must make the best choices. And this means that actors should study all of the play carefully to know the meanderings of the plot and its subtleties, and especially their character's function in it.

The opening scene of George Bernard Shaw's *Pygmalion* takes place outside the opera house at Covent Garden late at night after a performance. It's raining and there are no cabs. An older society woman sends her handsome young companion (Freddy) to fetch one. He bumps accidentally into Eliza, a ragamuffin flower girl, knocking the basket of flowers she's selling onto the wet pavement. Having overheard a part of their conversation, she loudly complains:

> **Eliza**: "Now then, Freddy, look where you're goin', dear." (Shaw's words in the script are spelled oddly to reflect a Cockney accent.)
>
> **Older Woman**: How do you know my son's name is Freddy, pray?
>
> **Eliza**: Oh, he's your son, is he? Well, if you'd done your duty by him as a mother should, he'd know better than to spill a poor girl's flowers.

In a production I saw, the actress read her second line above: "Oh, he's YOUR son, is he?" It makes perfect sense. However, there's a better reading: "Oh, he's your SON, is he?" The second interpretation is much richer in texture. Think about it. Older, rich woman; younger man. Eliza is thinking he's a gigolo. This immediately shows us a streetwise girl's reality and establishes her as a fighter who can fend for herself. Notice how she still berates the woman anyway. It also lets us know what Eliza thinks of the upper class. That's important since class strata in English society provide a major motif in Shaw's plot. And it's a clever and dynamic way to introduce the major female character and the young man who will become enamored with her later in the play. (And shows mastery of Shaw's structure as a playwright.)

Playwright. While discussing words, remember the creator of a play is not a playright, playrite, or even playwrite. A "wright" is a maker, builder. A cartwright builds carts; a wheelwright builds wheels. A playwright builds plays. He doesn't just "write" them. (But it's playwriting; not playwrighting.)

Actor Shelley Winters, in volume two of her memoirs (*Shelley II*) says she never truly "got" the full meaning of any role she played until she'd written, in her own handwriting, all her lines (preceded with the cue words). For her, this was certainly an extra layer of study, and it did provide an additional way of evaluating the words she'd be saying. Try it.

Director Father Gilbert V. Hartke: "Never overlook the intelligent impulse of an intelligent actor."

Despite the contributions of both playwright and director, it's more often the actor who finds the "truth" of the character and situation in ways that neither playwright nor director could have anticipated. This is logical when you think about it. After all, it's the actor who's playing the role. In the premiere production of my play *Wednesday's Children*, the actor, playing an uneducated and countrified village gossip during the WWI period, has a line referring to a local boy of dubious reputation who's fighting Germans in France: "Oh, he's probably over there parley vous-ing it up some French mademoiselle." The actor pronounced the last word as: madame-WAH-sul, suggesting she had probably seen the word but had never heard it said and wanted to impress everybody with her sophistication by knowing a little French. Although the character had very few lines, the actor's intentional mispronunciation of the word always got a huge laugh, guaranteeing the actor's and character's being remembered by the audience. In that one mispronounced word, the actor had defined her character and at the same time had remained totally true to the intent of the scene. She certainly made the scene and the play richer.

Tip # 23

Dealing with lines essential to the plot

One might say that all lines in a play are essential or else they wouldn't be there, but indeed playwrights spread out strategic information that the audience and indeed some of the characters must know in order that the dénouement (unraveling of the plot at the end) makes sense. In a mystery play, for example, the clues must be there, or the audience will feel cheated. I once heard of a small catastrophe when the director had to go on stage at the start of Act II and tell the audience: "I'm so sorry, but in the bank scene in Act I, Mr. Bramble left out the information that the real necklace is in the bank vault, and Mrs. Huntington-Smythe is wearing a paste copy."

It regularly amazes me when actors seem not to grasp this important element: that some of their lines are absolutely essential to the plot. In *The Sound of Music*, playwrights Howard Lindsey and Russel Crouse entrust very crucial information to nine-year-old Brigitta—information that changes the whole course of the plot and the lives of the von Trapp family. After Captain von Trapp has shown young Kurt how to dance the Laendler (by dancing it with Maria), Maria tells the children they must learn to like Frau Schraeder " . . . who's going to be your new mother." Brigitta, who never filters anything she says, replies: "Father's never going to marry her . . . he's in love with you. . . . And the way you looked at him just now when you were dancing. You're in love with him." Well, this is significant news! Maria has not even figured it out for herself. And she can't be in love with the Captain. She's going to be a nun. Furthermore, the Captain is ready to marry Elsa Schraeder.

In rehearsals for one of the productions I directed, the child actor playing Brigitta kept screwing up the lines in the scene—they were either late, paraphrased, or some of them weren't there. I finally had to have a long talk with her privately to help her understand the importance of accuracy and timeliness. She was fine in performance after she "got" it. Imagine hanging the plot burden of the second part of that play on the shoulders of a nine-year-old.

In this same vein is the awful situation that befalls an actor when he must respond verbally or take action to an important line (which has been left out). What does he do? He realizes an important part of the audience's understanding has been omitted. There have been all kinds of horror stories about scrambles backstage to get the left-out material back into the play in a later scene. And, of course, the worst scenario happens when nobody onstage realizes significant plot material has been omitted, and the public is left dumbfounded.

The play *Affairs of State* is a charming, frothy comedy. In the final three pages, there is a series of surprise turns and twists, involving each of the four major characters in different ways. It's a deft turn for playwright Louis Verneuil and leads to an enormously satisfying ending for the audience. After a performance, one of the actors in that scene came to me apologizing for having left out a line involving a delightful revelation about two steamship tickets. It did indeed muddy a complete understanding of the multi-leveled twists and turns, but the audience was so satisfied by the "happy ending" that nobody else ever asked, "What did a reference to the pair of tickets mean?"

Actors, it's always a good idea, in your initial study of a script to verify if you have lines that steer the plot. If you do, then highlight them in your script to remind you of their importance and be sure they don't get lost in performances.

Tip # 24

Handling overlapping lines and lines that "trail off"

In everyday speech, we talk "over" each other all the time. Can you imagine how stilted life would be if we had to wait to the end of every sentence in a conversation before responding. We'd be asleep very quickly. Ditto for a theatre audience. Actors in contemporary plays come up against this kind of thing often. When directors yell, "Pick up your cues," they are often suggesting just such an approach. Obviously, actors must know their lines completely (and without having to struggle for them) to be able to do this. Further, their diction must be clear so that audiences can understand and not wonder what is being said. Projection is important here. And there can be hazards like acoustics that make this difficult. I once saw a production staged in the gigantic waiting room of an old railroad station. With ceilings 30'-40' tall—and nothing to absorb sound—the technique was well-nigh hopeless. The sound reverberated around the room like an echo, and overlapping just didn't work.

The great acting team of Alfred Lunt and Lynn Fontanne are credited with this overlapping technique back in the 1920s. They were married in real life, rehearsed at home together, and just naturally developed this mode since they knew each other so well. At first, they were criticized because elocution and speech had been the primary traits of the acting stars of the past, not the realism we know in movement and voice today. The Lunts won.

The problem for actors is to know when the playwright intends this. Usually, a line with a long dash after it indicates it's a "cut-off" line, and the next speaker steps on the line so the conversation moves right along.

John: I told you I was not going to —

Mary: Oh, yes, you are, so don't give me any —

John: Who are you to tell me what to —

Mary: Oh, just forget it. I'm sick of the whole damn thing!

The playwright's intentions are pretty clear. Writer Aaron Sorkin in *The West Wing* gave us a master class in this kind of writing. To help his actors, he used parentheses in speeches to let them know where to begin to overlap:

Andy: It means (the demo is more than likely gonna crash).

Joanna: (over) You have to keep your voices down. Joel Pforzheimer is sitting out in the house.

21

In this instance, Joanna begins her overlap speech as Andy is saying "the demo." If a playwright has not provided a clear system to help actors, they might—with the advice of the director—work out their own pattern. Keep in mind that overlapping can add to believability, build tension in a scene, speed up the tempo of the play, give the voice more flexibility in dynamics, and involve the audience more directly. Win-win.

Lines that trail off: Sometimes, an actor will have a speech or line which indicates the character's hesitancy, pausing, or just not continuing, thus trailing off to nothing. The playwright usually indicates this intent by using three dots (periods) preceded by a space. Both the speaker and the listener in the scene have to know when this is the intent so they can get the timing right. For example:

> **Carole:** I'm afraid I . . . don't . . . handle death very well . . .
>
> **Jeffrey:** I guess none of us does . . . really.

In this exchange, Carole is dealing with a difficult topic and is hesitant and then just doesn't continue. The actor playing Jeffrey will need to time his response in order to allow Carole's statement to register with him and the audience. If the actor is really listening, he will feel when to reply. (And if the actor is very, very good, we might also learn his own view of Carole's position about death and if he agrees with it.)

Tip # 25

Listening

One of the things that separates the truly fine actors from the ordinary ones is the ability to listen. Often, inexperienced actors are so worried about what they must say that they don't listen to what others are saying. Their acting partners look them in the eyes and know immediately that "there's nobody at home." Nothing is happening in their heads. There's no communication—just the swap of words. Unhappily, it's often said of actors who've been playing a role for a long time, "Well, he phoned in that performance." It's not a flattering observation. It means he's gotten stale and is just "going through the motions." If there's been no connection with actors onstage, there's not likely to be a connection with the audience either. Learn to listen!

Michael Shurtleff: "Listening is not merely hearing. Listening is reacting. Listening is being affected by what you hear. Listening is active."

Tip # 26

Silence

Unless you are doing an evening of pantomimes, words are essential in theatre, and that means "sounds." We must also be aware, however, that sometimes the most magical things that happen occur when there is complete silence onstage. Many actors are terrified of stillness. Don't be. Trust that words may be only one avenue to communicate. Just watch from afar two lovers who are sitting on a park bench. You can't hear their conversation, but there's a whole story that can be derived from their smiles, touch, and total sense of oblivion about things going on around them.

In the film *Madame Curie*, actor Greer Garson, in the title role, has learned that her husband Pierre has been killed in a street accident. Instead of histrionics and melodrama, she remains quite still, the camera staying on her face for what seems like "forever." Her face quietly goes through the whole range of emotions, and we see the thoughts associated with them tumble through her mind. The Curies' life story is played out on her face in total silence. Of course, a camera close-up can show this in more detail than a stage version of it, but the point is: if the audience members are caught up in what you are doing, they'll follow you to the end. It works on the other side of the footlights, too. Perhaps the sincerest compliment actors get is that same silence in the audience during or after a scene.

> **Shelley Winters: "Every now and then, when you're on stage, you hear the best sound a player can hear. It's a sound you can't get in movies or television. It is the sound of a wonderful, deep silence that means you've hit them where they live."**

Tip # 27
Playing the Opposite

> **Michael Shurtleff: "Whatever you decide is your motivation in a scene, the opposite of that is also true and should be in it."**

Susan Lucci played the role of Erica Kane on the daytime drama *All My Children* for 41 years. Erica was a character you loved to hate. She was mercurial, unpredictable, and her machinations kept the people in Pine Valley on their toes—and usually riled up in some way. Why did the character stay in the story for 41 years when soap opera characters are regularly written out after their usefulness to the storyline is over? A huge part of the credit goes to writer Agnes Nixon who created the character, but Lucci, herself, found the elusive quality that actors want to achieve in their work—a rich and layered performance that included the opposite of whatever is really going on.

To get an idea of this duality, take Shakespeare's brilliant "Assume a virtue if you have it not!" scene between Hamlet and his mother Gertrude. He loves her dearly, but he is overwhelmed with disgust that soon after his father's untimely death she marries his father's brother, a man he hates. Hamlet is in torment, and we see his conflicting love and hate for her. In that case, however, the writer has given us the character's dueling opposites as a part of the plot. Mostly, actors on their own must find such disparate sides of a character they are building.

I was terribly discouraged several years ago when, at an early reading of my play, *Nocturne*, the actor playing my central character missed this concept entirely. The story is about a famous woman, an artist who has been blinded in an accident and has become embittered that she can no longer paint. The actor who played the part leaned heavily on an unrelenting "woe is me" note. There are many words in the script that suggest this, but I had not envisioned her that way at all. The character has a great sense of humor, no small amount of irony, and has no intention of succumbing to defeat, no matter what she says. Happily, in the productions I've seen, the actresses have found those opposites to create indelible finely-tuned and textured performances. This concept of opposites is one of the most difficult things actors ever have to do in their work. It takes enormous thought and vulnerability to achieve this duality successfully. And often it means getting out of your comfort zone. Oh, but what a difference it makes!

Jack Lemon: "If you really do want to be an actor who can satisfy himself and his audience, you need to be vulnerable."

Blocking/Movement

In the simplest terms, blocking is the transferring of the play from the page to the stage, putting the story on its feet—in action with real people (actors) moving now as the characters-come-to-life. It's a very, very important part of the rehearsal process. It involves the visual and the aural representation of the story— no longer the imagined characters on a page. It's the phase where the director guides the story, via the characters, telling the audience where to look and often what to feel. It has been said that a beautifully staged production (well-blocked) can be photographed for a still shot—at any given moment during the play—and we understand the story being told in the picture when we look at it. This means that the composition, mood, focus, etc. are telling the story through the visual. And of course, the words, the music, and the spectacle (sets, props, costumes, etc.) round out the whole experience. Directors work in different ways to block a play. Some use an improvisational method, based on actors' instincts, to create the visual story. There is an inherent problem with this method, however, because actors are more focused on their own parts and not the whole. Also, they are onstage and don't have a director's aesthetic distance. Most directors prefer to give specific blocking moves (which they've usually worked out in advance) because it's quicker, and actors like to know where they are on the stage when they say certain lines. It's an aid to memory, sequencing, and refining beat units (the smaller sections of the play that are book-ended by an entrance and an exit . . . or by dialogue or pantomime focused on a clearly-delineated topic.)

Tip # 28

Write down the blocking when given.

When blocking directions are given, write the notes legibly in the script where the movement occurs so you can read them later. Use a pencil with an eraser. There will be changes. Electronic devices may evolve as a better way to handle this, but the point is to write down the blocking as it is given to you by the director. I once directed a show where the leading man seemed never to remember his blocking. His acting mates were exasperated. At one rehearsal, I picked up his script thinking it was mine. There was not one note written in it anywhere! He probably thought he could remember it all. That was not realistic . . . and an unnecessary burden on the cast to have to deal with it.

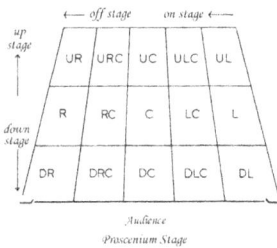

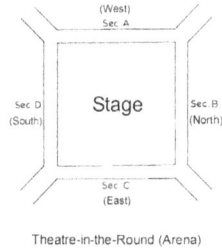

Proscenium Stage

Theatre-in-the-Round (Arena)

Remember, when actors are onstage, the directions given to them are from their point of view. For writing down blocking on proscenium stages, the above designations of the areas are helpful (XDC = cross down center, etc.). In arena staging, directors often give directions based on where groups of seats are (X to B = cross to section B of the seats, etc.). Geographical directions are another approach (X to N, cross to north, etc.). Another way is to imagine the stage as a clock (X to 9:20, etc.). No matter what system is used, it's important that everybody understands it and writes down the moves as they occur. While proscenium, thrust, and arena (in-the-round) stages are the most common, all kinds of spaces are being used today to stage theatre productions. The black box has gained wide usage since everything in the space (acting area and seating) can be arranged according to the director's concept and/or production demands.

Tip # 29

Keep the blocking consistent.

Once blocking for a show is set, it's important to keep it consistent. Other actors depend on it. Importantly, never change the blocking randomly without the prior knowledge of the other actors in the scene and the director or stage manager. At the final dress rehearsal (with an audience) of *Death of a Salesman*, which I directed, the character Ben entices Willy's son Biff into a sparring match.

When Biff is not looking, Ben trips him—standing over him with the pointed end of an umbrella, saying: "Never fight fair with a stranger, boy . . ." The actor playing Ben changed his blocking slightly and tripped Biff too early. The actor playing Biff fell improperly and broke his wrist. The production, a night away from opening, had to be postponed for a week while I found and rehearsed another actor in the role. It was an extra burden for the cast who had to rehearse with the new actor, a nightmare for the box office which had to undo/redo all the reservations, and a long-healing process for the original Biff. A cautionary tale.

Tip #30

Some basic rules for movement; theatre-in-the-round

Actors move generally while speaking their own lines, and usually on the least important ones. Why? To move on the lines of others is to take away the focus on the person speaking.

It's confusing to the audience and it's another classic way of upstaging. Remember to move before the line if the line is important; after the line if the action or business is the focus.

For many generations of actors, the set of rules about movement on proscenium stages has evolved, and these should be as Henry Higgins sings in *My Fair Lady:* " . . . like second nature to me now. Like breathing out and breathing in." You just do them without thinking. And yet, over and over, I've seen skilled, professional actors put themselves at a disadvantage by not paying attention to them. For example, you're seated in a chair facing the audience. To the left of you is a small table containing a telephone. It rings; you answer with your right hand since you're right-handed and favor that hand. No! You've unnecessarily closed off your body to the audience by crossing it with your right arm. You should answer with the left hand—which is logically closer to the phone anyway.

Similarly, you are standing, facing the audience, and you've been blocked to exit right, but you take your first step with your left foot. Once again, you've closed off your body. The rule: step off on the foot closest to the direction you're headed.

You've been blocked to kneel to propose to your fiancée. Kneel so the downstage knee is on the floor—otherwise you're closing off your body.

Often, when two characters are talking, a director will say: "Open it up a bit." She means to position your body so that the audience can see more of the front of you—and not you in profile. Two actors talking in profile for an extended time is very frustrating for the audience. They can't see either face well, and the voices are projecting to the wings—not outward.

In a scene with several people, all of whom are standing, you've been blocked to cross up left on a particular line.

Although it's closer to go behind a couple of the actors to get there, is that the proper way to do it? No! The audience loses you as you cross behind the actors, and that forces the actors to turn awkwardly to see you. If your cross takes you behind other characters who are seated, the rule changes. It may indeed strengthen the reason for the cross since you gain power by standing while others are seated. Obviously, there are exceptions to all these rules, if the text or concept so dictates, but they still serve, in a generic way, to keep the story clear and accessible to the audience. A dancer does not have time to think of the next step. The body must know it. In the same way, an actor's body must know these basic rules.

Blocking for theatre-in-the-round

Having directed in an arena theatre for four years, I learned very fast that there must be more movement so all four sides can see the action. Any reason to get an actor seated in a chair (or on the floor) was going to be helpful for sight lines. In this format, actors must know they are also acting with their backs. It's essential. The biggest aid for actors is a device called "twisting the pairs." Two actors facing each other in a scene must not "think" horizontal or parallel lines, but diagonal lines. Twisting body angles slightly opens up both bodies to being seen by more people. Most proscenium rules remain. It's just a different awareness.

Tip #31

Sitting

In everyday life, we sit so often and casually that we don't think about it. Onstage, however, the act of sitting becomes a considered part of an actor's technique and business.

In general, sit as the character would sit—based on his

age, the historic era, the costume, the kind of furniture, the time of day, etc. The women in *Downton Abbey* found they had no choice but to sit forward in a chair because of their confining corsets. Actually, they were well served by their undergarments because sitting forward demonstrated better posture, a sense of more interest in a conversation, and an "aliveness" in general. In drama schools, actors are taught, when they know they are to sit, to find the chair with the back of their legs—and sit without turning to see if the chair is there. That's just basic sitting, and it's still good advice. That approach is based on the understanding that when someone turns to look at something, we in the audience look to see what he's looking at. Consider the guy on the sidewalk who suddenly stops and looks upward. What does everyone around him do? In other words, there's no need to have the audience look at the chair. It interrupts focus.

I have found one of the weakest and less imaginative things actors do is to sit. More often than not, they sit as themselves, not as their characters. The writer, Havilah Babcock, in his delightful book, *I Want A Word*, chides would-be writers because of their lack of imagination in describing the actions of their characters. He illustrates this by quoting a simple sentence. "She came into the room." It's clear she entered the room, but that's all we know about the character. He then proceeds to use different verbs each of which lets us know much more about the character, her mood, and possibly what's been going on before she entered the room. Here are the verbs. Say the sentence aloud, using each and you'll get the idea: plodded, flounced, glided, trudged, breezed, strode, stalked, sidled, sauntered, strutted, marched, skipped, tramped, paced, toddled, staggered, waddled, shuffled, minced, pranced, strolled, hobbled, limped, slouched, sneaked, stamped, and wandered.

Using a comparable set of verbs, an actor might consider that how he sits reveals a great deal about his character (both before the action of sitting, and potentially what's going to happen afterwards).

Tip # 32

Think about how you look when sitting (the visual line).

You, the actor, have been blocked to sit on a sofa which is placed parallel to the footlights and your knees and legs are directly in front of you. Simple. All the audience can see you. Workable? Maybe not. What happens in this position is that the body is foreshortened—scrunched up—thus presenting a distorted proportionality. You could tend to look "flat" rather than three-dimensional. It's easily fixable by angling the legs in one direction or another. This slight angling provides a visual line from head to foot, providing dimension to the body. The position is particularly valuable for women who, in this era of very short skirts, must also consider modesty.

Plushy sofas and deep, upholstered chairs can look wonderful on a set, but they can also "eat you up" if you lean back for their comfort. You can quickly lose power and the aesthetics of the visual line. Ultimately, it's the director's job to monitor how you look and how best to capitalize on that look to help you in building your over-all character. Your knowledge, however, of "visual line" can be enormously helpful not only in plotting the physical characteristics of your character but also in situations where you don't have a director monitoring you—like in on-camera interviews. How you sit (and where) tells much. You'll rarely see a fashionably-dressed woman sit on a chair whose fabric clashes with her outfit or in a way than does not display her body well. Actors should always have that kind of awareness when they sit.

Tip # 33

Gestures

Have you ever been riding as a passenger in a car being driven by a person who is in a particularly bad mood when a car from behind swerves around your car at high speed and then cuts you off? The gesture given by the driver of your car, involving the use of at least one finger, is never produced in a namby-pamby fashion. It's direct, forceful, and graphic! No one misses the point! Gestures onstage are also an important tool for an actor, and they must carry the same conviction as the one coming from that angry driver. Think of it another way. The gesture might be a substitute for speaking. What would you say in place of the gesture?

As with the driving gesture, there's a bit of choreography involved: setup, execution, pay-off. It's got to have that complete arc of motivation-action to work. The problem for many actors is not realizing these three steps exist. Without them, the gesture can fall flat, be ineffective. Keep in mind that a gesture should be appropriate to the character (or not, for comic effect) and appropriate to the style of the play and to the time period. I have often heard a director tell an actor to get rid of the "penguin flips." This is a name for the half-hearted movement of hands (with elbows glued to the sides) that wants to be some kind of meaningful gesture but fails to communicate any real message. Any gesture in a play should logically arise from the text and/or character and be done with authority and conviction.

Tip # 34

Never upstage a fellow actor!

Upstaging is an ancient trick actors use to gain more attention for themselves. It gets its name from positioning on the stage. Two actors playing a scene where focus is equally divided between them (as well as the content of the scene) play on the same horizontal level—the audience seeing them equally. If one moves just a step upstage away from the audience, the other actor has to turn slightly away from the audience to look at his acting partner. The focus immediately goes to the actor upstage and we see more of the back of the other actor.

Upstaging can be done other ways, as well. *Auntie Mame* has a funny scene demonstrating this. The leading lady of a melodrama, Vera Charles, is emoting grandly—chewing up the scenery—while Mame (for whom Vera has gotten a job as an extra with a couple lines) steals the scene when her jangling bracelets get tangled in Vera's chinchilla coat. The eyes work faster than the ears, so unnecessary movement can upstage, draw away attention as well. Just remember, if you upstage someone, God may forgive you; your fellow actor certainly will not.

Lights

Actors almost never have anything to do directly with the lighting instruments that illuminate what they are saying and doing. Awareness of them, however, is very important.

Tip # 35

Are you in the light?

Stage lighting can do more than just illuminate the acting area. It can provide mood, atmosphere, and it can also make you look wonderful or just plain awful. The great Hollywood stars always knew where their "key" light was, the one that would give them every advantage in close-ups. None of these things is usually in an actor's province, but having a sense of how lights are designed in your scenes can be helpful.

It is not uncommon for lighting mishaps to affect your work. Occasionally, the lamp of an instrument will burn out during a performance, or an instrument can slip from its mooring on a pipe batten or light stand and its light goes astray. Or, horrors! A lighting technician goes to sleep at the console and misses a cue. Literally. (It's happened twice in my experience.) In several of these mishaps, I've seen even professional actors remain where they were originally blocked to be—an area now only in partial illumination. I always want to yell: "Adjust! Find the light!" (Actors know they are being properly lighted when they can "feel" the heat of the light on their faces. Always be aware of this!)

Another thing of which to be aware, particularly in film/TV work, occurs when the shadow of your head is blocking the light on the face of your scene partner. You're in a better position to notice this. Just move slightly to adjust. This kind of thing, by the way, points up a kind of duality for all actors. They are simultaneously themselves and the characters they play. Losing yourself in your character does not necessarily mean losing yourself, the actor. Your personal "tape" is always running on some level in the background.

Props

Actors often have an uneasy relationship with props since the wrong prop, a defective prop, or an absent prop can completely "undo" a performance. Here are some rules about props:

Tip # 36

Don't play with the props. Don't move props once they are set.

Never play with the props. Often, they are borrowed, or especially constructed for the production, and sometimes they are irreplaceable. Further, don't move props once they are placed onstage for a performance and on backstage prop tables.

Tip # 37

Get to know your hand props well. Think defensively about props.

If you must use a telephone in an important scene, and you discover the phone is missing once you are onstage—well, it's not a comforting feeling. Always check your props before a show, if possible. If there's no front curtain allowing for this, coming in before the house is open is worth the effort. The great French actor, Charles Boyer, playing in the Broadway production of *The Marriage-Go-Round*, always went onstage to check to be sure a cigarette lighter he would use was there—and working. No way would he put his "romantic lover" image in jeopardy by a missing prop or, heaven forbid, a faulty one.

In the Tyrone Guthrie Theatre production of *Foxfire*, when leading lady Jessica Tandy came for the first time onto the completed set, the home of her character, Annie Nations, she took quite a bit of time to pick up each object displayed on flat surfaces. She felt and examined each closely. It was her home, and she'd know the objects well. Did the audience need to know Miss Tandy did this? No, but the actress did. And she won a Tony and an Emmy for the role.

Actor Shelley Winters tells of an incident during the Broadway run of *A Hatful of Rain* involving props which forever changed her view of props in future plays. Her good friend and famed actor and acting teacher, Stella Adler, came to a performance one night, and mentioned afterwards that the scene where she was ironing a shirt did not work. Miss Adler then proceeded to put Miss Winters through a work session (till

2:00 a.m.) of ironing the shirt over and over (combined with the dialogue) until the scene was about the story and not about the shirt. Most everybody has ironed a shirt at some point or other. For the scene to work, the shirt had to be ironed almost robotically with the actor giving no thought to it while she was talking to someone about a very serious topic. The audience, however, saw a shirt being ironed by someone who didn't seem to have much knowledge about such things, therefore drawing their attention away from the dialogue and story. [By the way, Miss Adler's proper way to iron the shirt: first, the collar, then cuffs, left sleeve, right sleeve, the back, and then the front.]

Shelley Winters: "Your mind and words and intentions cannot be free until you are unconscious of the props and don't have to think about them."

Hair

Tip # 38

Discuss character hair styles early in rehearsals.

Do nothing with your hair, head, face or body unless you first talk to the director (or hair, costume, make-up designers, etc.)

There have been more near-murders in non-professional theatres over this issue on opening night than almost any other. Wanting to look spiffy at the first performance, actors often go to whoever cuts and/or styles their hair on the day of the opening and arrive at the theatre looking "very different" from the person the cast worked with the night before. Unfortunately, a hairdresser's "masterpiece" may or may not be anywhere close to the director's vision or appropriate for the character or to the time period of the play. This "no-no" would also extend to any adorned visible piercings (like nose and eyebrows, for example) or tattoos. **Repeat**: after being cast, do nothing to the hair—head and face—or body without first discussing it with the director.

Tip # 39

Be sure to test hairpieces under lights. Work with fake beards early.

In a production of *Camelot*, all the beautiful hairdos of King Arthur's England were carefully recreated for the ladies in the court. And then the ladies appeared on stage! Disaster. All the fake hair pieces stood out in stark contrast with the real hair. Light simply does not reflect off synthetics in the same way it does off real hair. Under gelled lights, it was worse. Some of the "brunette" hair turned red; some of the "blonde" hair, bluish. None of it could be used. Complete head wigs fare better but are more expensive. Period hairstyles are usually overseen by a hair designer, but be aware of this potential problem and test early.

Wearing fake facial hair additions (including false eyelashes) is never much fun—and they take time. Beards and moustaches must be created for the individual, each built to conform to the facial contours. There's the hassle of the adhesive to put on the pieces and then the gentle care to take them off—especially if they are to be used again. For the actor, "raw" skin and a possible allergic reaction to the adhesive are real. It's very wise to work with these pieces well before a public performance—and to verify if these pieces are the actor's responsibility to purchase, and where.

Even with all that kind of precaution, the unexpected can happen. In a lovely arena performance of *The Browning Version*, actor Bill Starrs, playing protagonist Andrew Crocker-Harris, became so moved in the scene where his young student gives him the gift of a copy of Browning's translation of *The Agamemnon* that he literally became teary-eyed. With a runny nose, no less. The fake moustache had held on tenaciously up to that point, and then it decided to part ways with his upper lip. Bill kept his index finger on the lip, hoping the moustache would re-stick, but it did not.

Remarkably, the audience, seeing what was happening, stayed with the scene. No titters or giggles. When Bill appeared at the curtain call, moustache now back firmly in place, there was an extra zip to the sustained applause. Afterwards, however, it was back to the drawing boards to figure out how to stave off that unforeseen problem before the next performance. Ergo, get started early when working with facial hair additions.

Costumes

Sutton Foster: "It's a bit of an outside-in approach, (but) clothing can reveal so much about a character."

Next to the director and choreographer, the costumer/designer is probably the next most important person on the creative team to make you look good on the stage. Literally! A designer/costumer must know a lot about art (color, composition, period, styles, etc.). In addition, there must be a knowledge of fabrics—textures, color fastness, how they "move," how they respond to light, how they "wear," how they are cleaned, what the costs are, and where to find them.

If the costumer is also a tailor or seamstress, then a whole new range of skills is needed: setting up a cutting board/worktable, using or creating patterns, cutting the fabric, knowing how to use a sewing machine efficiently . . . and handling zippers, buttons, trims, etc. It's both an aesthetic and a practical craft.

Tip # 40

Be gracious and friendly to the costuming staff.

You may know your body well, but the costuming staff are the experts about adorning it. In real life, you may not wear peplums or the color pink, but you are now a character in a play, and a play is not real life. Be cooperative. Be on time for measurements and fittings. They are just as important as rehearsals. In fact, they are rehearsals. Always hang up your costumes after a performance and be sure to designate which ones are to be cleaned. Never smoke or eat while in costume. Alienating a costumer by attitude, indifference, or mishandling costumes is the cardinal no-no in theatre. Do it, and you'll quickly discover why.

Tip # 41

Wear the proper shoes at fittings.

Always wear an approximation of the shoes you'll be wearing in the show. Height of heels for both men and women is super-important for accurate measurement for hems and cuffs.

Tip # 42

Ladies: foundation garments at fittings

Always wear the style of foundation garments you'll be wearing in the show. In an arena production of *Camelot* I directed, the Guenevere wore her every-day foundation garments for measurement-taking. All her gowns were made especially for her—fanned out to a group of talented seamstresses. A fortune was spent on elegant satins, silks, and fur trims, etc. At the first fitting, the actress wore a "Merry Widow" corset which was designed to cinch in the waist and push up the breasts. It was a very flattering hour-glass look. Unfortunately, the dresses hung on her like sacks. The seamstresses were understandably furious. All the costumes had to be altered, and the ladies never fully forgave her, thus creating an unnecessary chilliness backstage. Think. Be considerate.

Tip # 43

Ladies: rehearsal wear to personally own

All actresses should personally own a pair of black character shoes (often called "mary janes"). They are moderately heeled with a strap across the top of the foot. They are unobtrusive, and actually may be worn in many period productions when black tights or black hose and long skirts tend to make them disappear. These can come in handy on many occasions. In addition, all actresses should personally own black tights and black hose. They will get a lot of wear.

Tip # 44

Men: rehearsal wear to personally own

All actors should own a pair of wing-tip or plain black tie-up dress shoes. They can be used for many different periods. Wear them, when appropriate for a show, in rehearsals, too. Movement in them is very different from movement in today's ubiquitous athletic shoes. In addition, all actors should own a pair of over-the-calf black socks—not anklet-high socks. This avoids the bit of skin which can show above the sock when an actor sits and crosses his legs. Remember this especially for TV interview shows.

Tip # 45

"Work" the costumes.

Actors who've been around a long time get to play characters from all kinds of places and in different time periods—and they wear clothes nobody would wear today. Many actors have been known to say they didn't completely find their characters until they put on the costumes the characters wear. Wonderful costumes, themselves, can sometime become subtle (and sometimes, not so subtle) extensions of the characters who wear them.

Once you're in the costumes you are going to wear, "work" them. Go through the character's movements in the play, making them appear like normal everyday moments that fit the period of the play. You may find your posture has changed or that you sit differently. Know everything about a costume you wear and its function. Know how to work the hooks and buttons (and Velcro, etc.). Understand the "psychology" of the costume. An actor playing Sir Peter Teazle in *The School for Scandal*—with satin coat and lace at the end of the sleeves, knee pants, white stockings, and raised heels—is not likely to walk, stand, or sit like Stanley Kowalski in *A Streetcar Named Desire* or any of the characters in *Rent*.

In *The Belle of Amherst*, the monodrama about Emily Dickinson (1830-1886), the one long, white dress worn by Emily in the two-hour play becomes a character. Lines refer to it as being "bridal" white. While directing the play, I felt, when the costume had been completed, that a "dress" rehearsal was needed—a movement rehearsal (no lines) through the entire play. Actor Susan King had rehearsed in a nondescript, long rehearsal skirt from the costume closet to get the feel of the length of Victorian-era dresses. Suddenly, the real costume and its whiteness under lights gave the dress (and thus the character) a heightened importance.

Getting the draping of the skirt right every time Emily sat became especially important—and Emily sits in six different locations on the set, each requiring a different choreography for the dress. My goal was to be sure that any freeze-frame of the show/action would provide an aesthetic look in composition, balance, and focus. It was a two-hour rehearsal, constantly stopping and starting to refine each bit of movement. In one scene, Emily is kneeling in front of a loveseat imploring an unseen character seated there to see her as she really is. She is on one knee, with the other leg stretched out behind her under the "train" of the skirt. The audience's eyes, then, follow the dress from its train up her body and out her extended, outstretched arm. It is a beautifully evocative and aesthetic moment of entreaty with a Victorian "cameo" softness. But it is the costume which enhances the whole thing: the period, the story, the character, and ultimately the visual delight.

Audiences, of course, never know about this attention to detail. They want to see the tennis match; not the warm-up. They mostly assume the actor just does what she does on the spot, having no clue about the long hours of refining to make it all seem easy and effortless. And almost nobody understands, except those involved, the subtle interaction and working relationship between various members of the creative team, as in this case: writer, director, costumer, actor.

Generic Concerns

Tip # 46

Projecting: using your voice / mics

The ubiquity of body microphones today has been a plus and a minus. Having a sound technician monitoring what you say so that all members of the audience can hear you equally is definitely a plus, but actors before this technology learned how to project and fill up even the largest of houses. No doubt the great Ethel Merman (who dubbed herself "Iron Lungs Merman") would have been offended to be offered a microphone. Because actors nowadays are expecting to be using mics, training in voice production and projection has lagged. I think this is a mistake. Not every venue is going to have a marvelous sound system, and some places may have none. All acting programs have courses in speech that include a study of the vocal mechanism and how it works, the proper placement of the voice, pitch, intensity, phrasing, intonation, pronunciation, and indeed projection. In addition, there's the study of accents and regionalisms, and on and on. These are the preparatory things an actor needs to bring with him when he auditions.

In the eras when all the important Broadway actors toured their shows, the arrival at a "new" theatre would inevitably include the actors' testing of the acoustics in the house from the stage. They wanted a sense of how hard they'd have to work to fill it with their voices. That kind of thing has virtually died. There's at least one easy way, however, to help actors gauge how loud their voices must be in a performance space. Two actors, for example might test a scene by having one actor onstage and the other at the rear of the auditorium. They talk so each can hear the other well. It's often a shock at first. But at least they can get a sense of how the sound of their voices works in that space. They also learn how hard they are going to have to work to produce the volume needed . . . and how the body's vocal mechanism feels to make that projection. Remember we started off our tips with: "An actor must be seen, heard, and understood— if he is to be successful."

Tip # 47

Working with children and animals

Children. There is a very good reason why actors don't always like working onstage with children or animals. Audience attention always shifts focus to them—to see how good they'll be or if they'll mess up in some way. Or, simply for the audience to delight in the idea they're there at all.

As a director, I have learned to treat child actors as if they are adults—same rules, from day one of rehearsals. Happily, I have had no discipline problems. I think the children "got" the challenge "to be adults" and loved proving it. And the adult cast members enjoyed treating them as equals, even allowing that children will be children.

Actors working with older children need to be patient. Often the children are learning the craft at the same time they are creating a believable character. I encourage adult actors to be supportive, while at the same time remembering that Equity has strict rules about touch and keeping children safe and out of harm's way. Children merit respect. They are part of the ensemble, too.

Animals. I've worked with dogs and cats, and it's important to have their owners or trainers nearby. This provides a calming environment for the animals that are suddenly dealing with many new and different stimuli. I have only worked with cats that were held or carried by someone. I explained to the cats' owners what I basically wanted, and the owners coached actors in the best ways to handle the felines. And remember, only interact with animals on or offstage as blocked to do so. Keep it simple.

I "directed"—with no trainers being present—two different sheepdogs (as "Horrid") in two different productions of *Camelot*. In both cases, the actors playing King Pellinore (Horrid's owner in the play) befriended the animal, taking great pains to be kind and gain trust. The actors knew their own success depended on "man and beast" being in sync. King Pellinore (Pelly) makes his entrance with Horrid during the applause following the zesty ensemble number, "The Merry Month of May." Lots of people; lots of noise. The ensemble stays onstage during the brief scene with Pelly and Guenevere. I wanted the dog to know what to expect. In both productions, the dogs were on leashes held by Pelly. My biggest concern was how the dogs might react to audience responses. I needn't have worried because both dogs "got into character" after a few rehearsals and performed beautifully. The swell of applause when Pelly and Horrid entered for curtain calls was clear testament to their success—and I give credit to the actors who handled the dogs. I was amused when the owner of Hermes de la Galliard (the first Horrid) told me Hermes dutifully sat by the front door at 8:00 p.m. each night for a week after the show closed, waiting to go to the theatre. Ah, when the acting bug bites . . .

Tip # 48

Don't telegraph the ending.

Audiences don't like predictability in characterization, plotting, or in dénouements. The fun is "getting there" . . . and being both surprised and satisfied. And occasionally, even galvanized into action. In murder mysteries, we don't like to figure out the culprit in the first ten minutes. We like being our own detectives.

In an episode of *Murder, She Wrote*, actor and producer Angela Lansbury had to admonish a young actor (whose character was the guilty party in a particular episode) not to give away the answer to whodunit. The actor was playing the ending.

Remember: The actors know the whole plot.

The characters do NOT. They are living the story as it happens, and do not know where it's going. They always start a scene "in innocence."

If a director tells you that "you know too much," he means you're playing the actor's knowledge of the ending—not the character's next unknown moment.

Tip # 49

Create a backstory.

Actors, your job, always, is to create a convincing and believable character.

I once asked an actor what church his character attended. He replied, "I have no idea." "Why not?" I continued. The audience does not know this (unless it's mentioned in the script) and potentially doesn't care, but if the actor knows what the character's religion is, he might say the line: "I don't drink." very differently as an Episcopalian from the way he'd say it as a Baptist. Write a short biography of the character. Here are some things you might consider:

Does he look like me? If not, in what ways is he different?

How does he speak? (Fast? Slow? With an accent? etc.)

Does he speak any foreign languages? Which ones?

How does he walk? What's his posture like?

What's his favorite food? Movie? Song? Hobby? etc.

What does he do for a living (if not explained in the script)?

What are his quirks?

Is he musical? Dance? Sing? Play a musical instrument?

Is he an optimist? Pessimist?

Does he have a sense of humor?

What kind of books does he enjoy?

What do the other characters think of him?

What animal is he most like?

For specific scenes, you might also evaluate these: What was the character doing before he came into the scene. Does any of that activity (or result of it) show in the scene? Where is he going when he leaves?

I once heard the great actor Hume Cronyn speak in Minneapolis about how he had built his character Harpagon in the Tyrone Guthrie Theatre's production of Molière's classic, *The Miser*. He said, "The character is always grasping for more money, pulling it towards himself. I immediately thought of a crab with its long claws reaching out and turning inward." (Harpago means "hook.") And, indeed, he used that crab allusion in his body movements throughout the play. He wore a black, graduation-type gown, knee-length pantaloons, and white stockings. His outstretched, flailing arms presented the image of "gimme, gimme." It was a successful visual combination of animal image, costume, and character trait.

In her book, *Seven Steps to Children's Creative Dramatics*, Pamela P. Walker uses a variation of this in helping to build the physical aspects of a character. She is working with children, of course, but the concept works with any age. She divides the body into three horizontal sections (or spheres): head and neck, trunk (heart, midsection), and legs and feet. Characters can be built that have traits of each of those spheres.

Head and neck person—The voice is light and airy, hands and arms are feathery, and walking is on tip toes.

Such a character might be Glinda, the Good Witch in *The Wizard of Oz*.

Trunk (heart and midsection) person—The voice is forceful, hands and arms move with vigor and purpose, and walking is on the balls of the feet. These are the hero characters: James Bond, Annie Sullivan, Tarzan, Robin Hood, Atticus Finch, etc.

Legs and feet person—The voice is low and deep, hands and arms hang heavy, and legs and feet are earthbound. Think Marlon Brando in *The Godfather* or bear and ogre characters in children's fiction.

Tip # 50

Photos—head shots, PR shots, and production photos

With the ubiquity of cellphones, almost any kind of photo can be made "on the spot"—even reasonably-good résumé head shots. And with a good printer and photo-stock paper, reproduction can be very quick. All actors must deal with being photographed. It just goes with the territory. Well-done photos work in positive ways. A good head shot will help you be remembered. (Have both black and white **and** color ones). Good rehearsal photos in print media can help build an audience. Good production photos become valuable "history." Usually, actors have nothing to do with the photography arrangements, but whenever possible, it's important to be proactive and try to assure you are photographed "at your best." The superb photos of great photographers like George Hurrell, Yousuf Karsh, and Annie Liebovitz not only captured a well-lit and "staged" subject, but they also captured a sense of motion and something going on behind the eyes. There was an aura, mystique. It was artistry at its best. It's very hard to find a superb **theatre** photographer. Most photographers don't understand that the best photos show the actor(s) **in character while performing**. To pose a group and then say, "Hold it!" reflects little "life" and no "action." Dull. Scenes of characters in the action work best. Some photographers routinely use a flash and therefore wash out the stage lighting effects. Their photos do a disservice to lighting designers and directors who've worked to create mood and atmosphere.

The call for production photos usually takes place after a performance once the show is up and running. The director or his designee has usually prepared a list of those photos to be made, working from the end of the play backwards to Act I. This activity is, like a tech rehearsal, long and tedious, involving costume and set changes. Cooperation from actors is essential. Photographers (and crew members who are busy changing sets, lights, and props) will love you if you are cheerful, stationed where you need to be for the next photo (in the correct costume), and don't talk.

Tip # 51

Health is the # 1 priority.

Have you ever had to do a Sunday matinee in a two-character show when your onstage acting partner had a hangover from too much partying the night before? Everything about your performance can go down the tubes very fast. For all actors: your body is your "instrument." Would you really like to spend two hours at a violin recital when the violin is out-of-tune?

Proper rest and a healthy diet will not only help you sharpen your performance, but they'll endear you to your colleagues because **you'll be <u>there</u> for them in <u>their</u> performances** when they are working with you.

Jennifer Hudson: "Gaining control over your health and well-being is one of those times in life that you get to be completely selfish and not feel bad about it."

Beyoncé: "Be healthy and take care of yourself, but be happy with the health and things that make you, you."

Tip # 52

Practice etiquette and good manners.

It's all about the golden rule: "Do unto others as you would have them do unto you." You will be judged by your talent, but you'll also be judged by the way you handle yourself, often in trying situations. Most backstage areas are cramped and hardly glamorous. Your conviviality and patience will be tested.

In rehearsals of that Broadway production of *The Front Page* mentioned earlier, a young actor missed his cue because he was in the theatre basement with some other actors watching the World Series on TV. Star Robert Ryan was not pleased. When it happened the third time, Ryan threatened to walk. Not only was the young actor rude, but one could legitimately wonder if he was serious about a career in theatre.

Almost all actors take and note directions on their cell phones. The phones are usually close at hand and it's quick and easy. The problem comes when actors are on social media during rehearsals—sometimes taking photos and posting them. This is not only disrespectful to the director and cast, it's more and more illegal, actors being required to sign nondisclosure contracts about social media.

Many theatres, particularly dinner theatres, have the cast to line up in a receiving line in the lobby after a performance to greet the audience as they leave. Actors occasionally gripe about this, but that attitude is short-sighted. Promotion, publicity, and PR are a part of the business in the acting profession. Being gracious to the audience can be fun, good for you and your career, and who knows? You might meet somebody fabulous and get invited to dinner.

There are likely to be newspaper and TV interviews (always at ungodly hours). Accept them with grace, as long as they don't interfere with the work/show. Be charming, promote the show, and gin up interest to fill the seats. Isn't that what you've been working towards?

There's no more laudatory compliment than, "If _____ is available, get her for the show. She's absolutely wonderful to work with." Translation: she's talented, a pro, and a trouper. Always leave a production with producers and directors wanting to work with you again.

Curtain Calls

As we talk about etiquette, we can't omit mention of curtain calls. Manners matter there, too. The curtain call is simply a time for the audience to acknowledge the actors for their performances. Artistically, the province of curtain calls is the director's, and she plans, blocks, and rehearses them as she would any other part of the play. And the order of the bows attaches to the importance of the roles and the actors who play them—starting with the chorus or small roles working up to the leads who appear last. In arena stages, the calls are very much "choreographed" since actors are bowing to all sides in continual movement. Sometimes, directors block curtain calls with actors still in character for, perhaps, some delightful effect. Sometimes, directors elect to omit curtain calls, especially if they want to leave the message of the play as the last thing seen and remembered.

Occasionally, actors, in their enthusiasm, forget to stick to the rehearsed calls and embellish these moments. In a production of *Come Blow Your Horn*, an actress appeared nightly in the group calls wearing glamorous dresses she had not worn in the show. In a college production of *The Crucible*, the leading actor (a religion major) was so carried away he thrust his arm high in the air with raised index finger (symbolizing "One God"), causing a mutiny among the cast. At an Atlanta production of *Camelot*, actor Richard Harris (who'd also starred in the film version) came on last, took his bows, and then held up his hands for quiet while he announced, to much acclaim, the score of the Atlanta Braves ballgame which had been going on at the same time.

Let joy and enthusiasm reign for sure, but actors should always be aware that curtain calls should reflect the same professionalism expected of the play itself.

Tip # 53

Know theatre history and its literature.

I once asked a college musical theatre major to go and prepare a list of the roles he could realistically play from the long list of "classic" Broadway musicals. He was slightly built and had an excellent tenor voice. He had access to a large collection of libretti, recordings, and films. He came back in a very short time. "I can't do this?"

"Why not?" I asked

"I've never read the shows. I've seen some of the movie versions, and heard the cast albums of a lot, but . . ."

This was quite a revelation to him. He had focused on

Broadway songs, not the plays, not the history, nor had he seen many musicals onstage. "Broadway" was some sort of amorphous realm which equated to: bright lights, glamour, fame, money, and success.

It's always puzzled me that among the hundreds of actors I've worked with, there've been very few who have shown any curiosity about the history, the evolution, and the eras of this wonderful thing we call "theatre." It's always about performing, or about productions, or about theatre lore. And the biggest unspoken truism among actors is how few plays they've actually read. Titles and names of playwrights get bandied about in conversation—with great enthusiasm as if there's some intimate, first-hand knowledge—but a real knowledge of theatre literature may reside only among the academics and the critics. Naysayers might say: "But plays are meant to be seen before an audience. True. But plays are also literature. Reading a play a week is not an unreasonable goal if you are serious about acting.

We expect our doctors to have at least "read up on" medicine. Would we go to a lawyer who's only **seen** trials on TV and in the movies? And yet, we don't have any similar expectation about actors. The naïve (and there are lots of them) think they can get up onstage and say memorized lines like the actors they see. I often hear someone say, "I think I'm going to write a play." All of this, of course, without any awareness of the amount of time and study it takes to perfect these crafts.

In truth, actors don't need a wealth of book-learning about theatre. Their bodies, voices, intelligence, wit, imagination, and way with words are their "staples." Would they be better knowing the history of theatre and having read lots of plays? I think they would. They'd give richer performances because they'd know more about traditions, influences, patterns of social behavior—and especially get to know the plays considered important in their own times. They'd bring more to the table. And don't we want to experience more than the average/mundane/clichéd when we go to the theatre?

Superstitions

A part of theatre history and its lore are the superstitions that persist from generation to generation. "Don't say 'Good luck!' That brings **bad** luck. Say, "Break a leg!" instead. Oddly, the "leg" referred to here is not a human leg, but a side curtain, placed onstage to hide the backstage areas. So, "breaking a leg" literally means the moment you set foot in view on a stage.

"A bad dress rehearsal will bring forth a great opening night." (Oh, how we like to believe that!)

And, it's heresy in a theatre to mention Shakespeare's Scottish play by name. (Sorry, *Macbeth*.)

"Never whistle backstage!" In olden days, that was valuable advice since a whistle backstage was a way for stagehands to communicate with each other about lowering drops and scenery. You might have been flattened.

These are all harmless, of course. Enjoy them for what they are: treasured actors' traditions.

Tip # 54

Be *realistic* about a *fantasy* world.

Rejection in the performing arts is legendary—and very public. The world of theatre is not for the faint-of-heart. Many actors will tell you they've been rejected more at auditions than they've gotten parts. It's unsettling, disappointing, and it hurts. We are our own "instruments."

Sometimes a rejection for a part can seem like a rejection of us, the human beings.

We respond with: "I was far better than she was." "He gave a crappy audition." Or, "I bet there's a casting couch around somewhere." And on and on. At least, it's a way to vent.

The difficult thing about this is that we have to start all over again each time we audition. Even famous actors have to audition—as did Angela Lansbury for *Mame* and Marlon Brando for *The Godfather*. And so it is for singers, dancers, comedians, and even playwrights. Robert Anderson (*Tea and Sympathy*) once told me he had to start at the bottom to "shop" every new play—and he'd already had several hits on Broadway.

Remember: It's NOT about you!

If you aren't cast, this is not a commentary on you or your talent. The director simply has another vision of the role than the one you present. It can be about looks, voice, height, weight, etc. Indeed, you may be the best actor in the room, but not for that role in that production. So, relax!

Jennifer Hudson: "It can be a real struggle to accept that sometimes appearance can be more important than talent or intelligence."

Don't think of an audition where you are not cast as wasted time. It's not infrequent to hear a comment like: "Wouldn't she be great if we were doing *Carnival!*" And guess what show gets on the roster for next season . . . and who is being thought of as the lead? Directors remember a great audition—even it's not for the show they are currently casting. Also, for the actor, if you are new/unknown at the theatre doing the casting, it's a way to be introduced. **Moral**: There will always be auditions. Some will be winners; some, losers. When there's a loser, grab a friend and go have a drink. When there's a winner, throw a party.

Lin-Manuel Miranda: "Every day has the potential to be the greatest day of your life."

Tip # 55
Thank-you notes are a must.

We live in a society and an era where thank-you notes are becoming increasingly "quaint." Not even for wedding gifts, the absence of which used to be the ultimate faux-pas in social propriety. One can blame a lessening of manners in general and perhaps a generation of hand-held communications devices where pen and paper have become relics of the past. Even cursive writing is no longer taught in some schools.

Actor Edward Marshall has told me that, as a courtesy, he always writes thank-you notes to the producer and director of whatever show or acting gig he's been working on. He is certain that this simple gesture has aided him in being cast again in other projects by the same folks. People remember a hand-written note and the courtesy of a "thank-you".

Once, when I was working on a production of the musical *American Beauty* in a university setting, a fine pianist/composer from the music department was assigned to accompany the show. The theatre students didn't know her or her background—or how lucky they were to have someone of her caliber supporting them musically. I mentioned this to them quietly and suggested it might be nice to thank her occasionally. She really was doing the group a favor. They "got" it . . . and always made a point as they individually left each evening to go by the piano and thank the lady. The pianist blossomed, telling me she'd never gotten thank-yous like that from the music students she accompanied. The production took on a gentle warmth among the cast, making it one of those special theatrical experiences of a career. Remember that such acknowledgments are always appreciated by choreographers, music directors, etc. when they are working at rehearsals to make you look good.

Sometimes, the lack of a thank-you note can have a far-reaching effect. A husband-and-wife couple I know started a tradition of giving an annual, substantial scholarship to an outstanding theatre major at his alma mater, driving to the campus to present the award in person. When they noticed after several of these, they were not getting thank-you notes, (or acknowledgments of any kind), they paused to reconsider whether to continue the annual gift. The recipients had no clue that their thoughtlessness might affect other students in the future.

I still believe that nothing less than a hand-written note in first-class stamped postal mail is really appropriate. A phone call is nice, but it should be in addition to the mailed note. An email, text, or a tweet? Well, they might acknowledge appreciation, but they'd have no "class"—no gravitas. Why diminish the gesture of thanks? Some of my actor friends who read drafts of this book suggested I was whistling in the wind to include this advice to actors about a hand-written thank-you letter, but I shall stick to it. There's nothing to lose and everything to gain in expressing appreciation and thanks. Everybody feels good. And there's an actual keepsake letter to hold on to and possibly re-read from time to time. Win-win.

"Class"

I mentioned the word "class" above. It's not something you can buy, borrow, or steal. Either you've got or you haven't. Asked to define the word, I always tell the story of my friend, the brilliant costumière, Sara Stewart. She was designing costumes for one of those productions of *Camelot* I directed. I chose a different look from the Broadway production, a color palette she was not convinced of. She invited me to accompany her when she bought the fabrics for Guenevere's and Arthur's costumes. I helped pick them out and approved all of them. At the costume parade before opening, I was horrified when two of Guenevere's dresses moved—and she didn't. The fabric was too heavy and had almost no possibility for movement or draping. I knew they wouldn't work, and that I'd have to say so. After the actors left, and we were alone, she said, "I wonder if you'd mind if I re-do two of Guenevere's dresses," and she cited the two. Instead of making me wrong—which I was, she just "got on with it" . . . and I was grateful, and she knew I was grateful. No drama. A class act—and a pro.

Exit

Writing this book has been fun, especially as I have remembered instances which illustrated my points. Actors always want to look good and make their characters convincing. This involves trust in the director who is consistently in evaluation mode, mulling over what to keep and what to jettison. It's been a great pleasure over the years collaborating with probably over a thousand actors, watching them achieve heights and successes they sometimes didn't know they were capable of. Their successes have been mine, too, and for that, I am very grateful. There's a wonderful line in William Marchant's play, *The Desk Set*, which says: "If I didn't work here, I'd pay to get in."

I'd particularly like to thank my merry band of theatre buddies who read drafts of this book and made valuable suggestions: Michael Burgess in Toronto, Barbara Burton in Chicago/Evanston, Jimmy Hicks in Richmond, Randy Noojin in New York, and Kay and Neil St. Claire in Asheville. Among them are five actors, three directors, a playwright, a choreographer, a pianist, a librarian, a founder of a community theatre, an Equity Stage Manager, two university professors—one, the chairman of a university theatre department, and the artistic director of a theatre company. Lucky me.

Some years ago, I had the great privilege of directing the late actor-director-author Ron McIntyre-Fender in several productions. He had a remarkable gift of surrounding people in his orbit with love and support. Audiences adored him. In addition to his thespian skills, he was a sly humorist and a wily raconteur. When needed, he had a rubber face and a facile way with accents that would hold people in delighted thrall. I'd like to end with a story he often told, summing up, in a nutshell, what acting and theatre are. I asked my long-time friend and kindred-spirit, actor Susan King, to recall it:

When asked repeatedly how he approached a role, Ron replied that he didn't have a specific method, he just did a deep study of the character and put himself in the hands of good directors to guide him. But that didn't satisfy whoever was asking the question. So, Ron finally broke down and, in his best countrified dialect, said:

"Well, first you go to play practice and the lady gives you yer playbook so you can learn yer part

by heart. Then you go to play practice for a long time so the lady can tell you whar to stand and whatnot. And then, after you go to play practice for a long time and you know yer part by heart, all you have to do is act like you was really thar. Like it was really happnin' to you."

And so, dear friends, let me wish that you'll be able to " . . . act like you was really thar. Like it was really happenin' to you." Break a leg!

Judy Garland: "Always be a first-rate version of yourself rather than a second-rate version of somebody else."

Acknowledgments

While the materials I reference in this book are in public domain or covered by fair use, I would especially like to acknowledge the writers: William Shakespeare, George Bernard Shaw, Arthur Miller, Alan Jay Lerner, Howard Lindsey and Russel Crouse, Harold J. Kennedy, Aaron Sorkin, William Marchant, Havilah Babcock, and Hume Cronyn. And I'm grateful for the remembrances of Collin Wilcox and Susan King as well as the excellent insights of author/teacher, Pamela P. Walker.

For those who like reading actors' memoirs, I recommend these books (mentioned in the text) which speak to the practical aspects of acting and are delightful "reads": *A Terrible Liar* by Hume Cronyn (William Morrow and Company, 1991); *No Pickle, No Performance* by Harold J. Kennedy (Berkley Publishing Corporation, 1977); and *Shelley II*, by Shelley Winters (Simon and Schuster, 1989).

Judging from the many actor quotes that float around the Internet, it's easy to guess that audiences and readers also enjoy actors talking about their elusive and often-mysterious craft. For the quotes used here, I am grateful to: Harrison Ford, John Kander, James Earl Jones, Amy Schumer, Olivia Colman, Steve Martin, Kim Cattrall, Stephen Sondheim, Paula Abdul, Father Gilbert V. Hartke, Michael Shurtleff, Shelley Winters, Jack Lemon, Sutton Foster, Jennifer Hudson, Lin-Manuel Miranda, Judy Garland, Beyoncé, and Meryl Streep.

For every actor the audience sees onstage, there're probably two or more unseen folks helping to make the play happen and to make all the actors look good. The same is true with writing. No play or book just happens for an author without unseen support. In all my writing, I'm incredibly grateful to have the unflagging TLC of Wes Heath, who is simultaneously reader, critic, devil's advocate, IT geek, and cheerleader—not to mention talented editor/advisor and designer of the cover of this book. Graçias, merci, danke!

Meryl Streep: "The formula for happiness and success is just being actually yourself, in the most vivid possible way you can."

Some popular plays by C. Robert Jones.....

Nocturne

A winner of Theatre Memphis's National Play Contest (premiering under the title *Chiaroscuro*), this two-character comedy-drama tells the story of famous artist Sara Canfield, a white transplanted southerner living in New York City, who is blinded in an accident and can no long paint. Becoming isolated, she seeks a reader who will come in for two hours a day. Enter Raymond Gordon, a streetwise young black ex-con. The friction is immediate, and the interplay of these two fractured lives provides the fabric of the play. As the layers are peeled away, the discoveries are often surprising. "A clever and nicely-balanced story about two people with the potential to improve each other's lives." *Detroit Free Press*; "The script is quick-paced, unpretentious, and one of its greatest strengths is the tension it builds." *The* (Memphis) *Commercial Appeal*

Taking a Chance on Love

This delightful comedy was the winner of the National ScriptWorks Competition of the Southern Appalachian Repertory. It introduces three generations of the dynamic Rutledges of Charleston. Newspaper editor Edgar is weighing an offer to sell the family's 80-year-old newspaper. He and his mother, Margaret, are the major shareholders, and his two ex-wives, Roxana and Adele, also are part owners. He invites them all to a weekend gathering at the Rutledge home to make a decision and to celebrate the engagement of son, Ned, to fiancée, Madeleine, whom none of them has met. When it turns out that Madeleine is French—and nearly as old as Ned's mother, Roxana—things turn topsy-turvy. Then arrives

Solange, Madeleine's sexy daughter, who makes a play for Edgar, who's busy being smitten again with wife number two, Adele. Midst of all this, Cupid's arrow catches 75-year-old Margaret totally unaware when Madeleine's ex-husband, Kiki, arrives and falls madly in love with her. Everybody is in love with somebody else on stage, but not necessarily the "logical" person. "... an engaging script, full of humor and insight. *Taking a Chance on Love* features lovable, zany characters who, for all their foibles, do follow their hearts. The result is entertaining and satisfying." *Asheville Citizen-Times*.

JUDGEment

This play's big question: Is there nobody left in Washington, DC who'll stand up and say "NO!"? Kay Yerby doesn't think so. She's the wife of Dan Yerby, Chairman of the Senate Judiciary Committee, and she's fed up. Kay opts for action when she sees her husband pushing the Committee to confirm Judge Garrett Ridley, a nominee for the Supreme Court—even though the process is stalled when Judge Ridley is accused by Dr. Regina Lazarus, of sexual assault when they were in college. Kay feels the judge is unfit. If she can persuade three senators (one being her husband) to change their votes, Ridley's confirmation will fail. This is crucial. Otherwise, there'll be a conservative majority. She finds two senators who might be amenable-and invites their wives to tea. Thus begins the plan to upset the craven desire (and machinations) to bold onto power. Can integrity be restored in DC high places? Can the three women make it happen? The play explores if not an ideal world, the possibility of a better one.

info@robertfreedmanagency.com

Also by C. Robert Jones

I Like It Here!
The Wild and Wonderful World of Theatre

Whether it was the opening night of *Breath of Life* with Judi Dench and Maggie Smith in London, or the preBroadway opening of Carol Channing's *Hello Dolly!* in Washington, D.C., or experiencing Laurence Olivier and Vivien Leigh in *Macbeth* at Stratford-upon-Avon, C. Robert Jones has enjoyed a lifetime of adventures as actor, playwright, director, teacher, composer, and avid theatre-goer, adventures that have taken him to fascinating places filled with fascinating people.

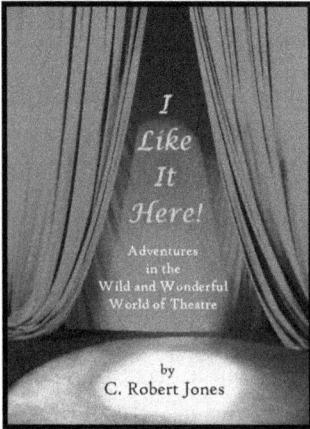

I Like It Here! relates these stories, along with many others, and also tells the backgrounds of several world-premiere productions he directed: Bernard Sabath's *You Caught Me Dancing*, Steve Bouser's *Senator Sam*, and his own musical, *The Clown*. It's a charming slice of theatre in the U. S.

Available from Pisgah Press at www.pisgahpress@gmail.com, Amazon.com, barnesandnoble.com

Aha!
"Eureka" Moments That Changed My Life

Have you ever had one of those sudden enlightening moments when things "come together" and you "get it"? We all have. The dictionary calls them "aha moments." C. Robert's latest book, *Aha!": Eureka Moments That Changed My Life* chronicles some of those major those moments when, with no warning, his life headed off in some unforeseen direction because of an invitation to an audition, a phone call, a letter, a badly-phrased (and misunderstood) question, a request to direct "the worst play I ever read" . . . and more. His discovery of these moments provides anecdotes

"Aha!"

'Eureka' Moments
That Changed My Life

by
C. Robert Jones

of surprise, humor, and humility, and it's full of delightful people who played significant roles along the way. The book is written in a light, breezy style, it's full of photos, and makes for a delightfully fun read.

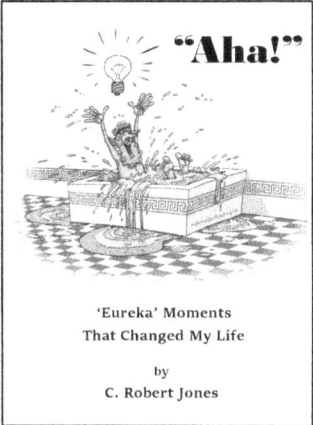

Lanky Tales

The Remarkable Adventures of Lanky Lonegan

This collection of four books grew out of a character C. Robert Jones first developed for his musical *A Belonging Place*, in which a country story-teller makes up stories about Lanky Lonegan, a character designed to amuse three local children during long winter nights. More stories appeared in the

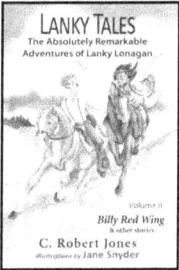

LANKY TALES
The Absolutely Remarkable
Adventures of Lanky Lonagan

Volume II
Billy Red Wing
& other stories
C. Robert Jones
illustrations by Jane Snyder

play's sequel, *Wednesday's Children*, and Jones brought Lanky to life as an onstage character in his one-act play, *The Blabbermouth* (www.dramaticpublishing. com). Ever since, readers and theater-goers, both adults and children, have appreciated the tales' country flavor, moral uprightness,

67

and the character of a boy who constantly screws up while trying—and eventually succeeding—to make things better.

LANKY TALES
The Absolutely Remarkable Adventures of Lanky Lonagan
Volume III

A Good and Faithful Friend
& other stories

C. Robert Jones

Imagine a 13-year-old boy who's already six feet, four inches tall and you'll know how Laurence Lonagan got the nickname "Lanky." It's 1913, long before radios, television, or computers existed, and even telephones and automobiles are still rare in the small mountain town of Claggett Cove where Lanky lives with his widowed mother.

Lanky's adventures always seem to happen when he tries to help someone in trouble, or when he gets a well-intentioned idea to make a bad situation better. And then . . . wham! Things go horribly wrong. But by using his clever, quirky, and often humorous way of looking at things, Lanky saves the day and, in the end, all ends well.

Throughout the Lanky Tales, citizens of Claggett Cove appear in story after story: a Scottish immigrant who owns the general store, a well-meaning preacher whom Lanky rescues more than once from some impending disaster; a hermit whose life Lanky saves during a blizzard; the choir director who can't sing well; a Cherokee who saves the village from a terrible epidemic; and, of course, Lanky's "Maw," who helps guide him to do the right thing. Lanky himself is always curious, full of fun, and eager for adventure.

Notes

Also available from Pisgah Press

Gabriel's Songbook   Michael Amos Cody
$17.95   FINALIST, FEATHERED QUILL BOOK AWARD, FICTION, 2021

A Twilight Reel   Michael Amos Cody
$17.95   GOLD MEDALIST, FEATHERED QUILL BOOK AWARD, SHORT STORIES, 2021

Letters of the Lost Children: Japan—WWII   Reinhold C. Ferster
$37.95   & Jan Atchley Bevan

Musical Morphine: Transforming Pain One Note at a Time   Robin Russell Gaiser
$17.95   FINALIST, USA BOOK AWARDS, 2017

Open for Lunch   Robin Russell Gaiser
$17.95

Shade   H. N. Hirsch
$22.95

The Last of the Swindlers   Peter Loewer
$17.95

Reed's Homophones: A Comprehensive Book of Sound-alike Words   A.D. Reed
$17.95

Swords in their Hands: George Washington and the Newburgh Conspiracy   Dave Richards
$24.95   FINALIST, USA BOOK AWARDS, HISTORY, 2014

Trang Sen: A Novel of Vietnam   Sarah-Ann Smith
$19.50

Invasive Procedures: Earthquakes, Calamities, & poems from the midst of life   Nan Socolow
$17.95

Deadly Dancing   THE RICK RYDER MYSTERY SERIES   RF Wilson
$15.95

Killer Weed   RF Wilson
$14.95

The Pot Professor   RF Wilson
$17.95

To order:

Pisgah Press, LLC
PO Box 9663, Asheville, NC 28815
www.pisgahpress.com

www.ingramcontent.com/pod-product-compliance
Lightning Source LLC
Chambersburg PA
CBHW060417050426
42449CB00009B/1995